How Come...? Easy Answers to Hard Questions

How Come...?
Easy Answers to Hard Questions

By Joyce Richards

Illustrations by Susan Perl

Platt & Munk, Publishers/New York

This book is created from the award-winning advertising campaign for Health-tex clothes in response to requests from parents and educators throughout the country.

Contents

Who thought up spaghetti? 8

Why is the ocean salty? 9

Why do birds sing? 10

What is a falling star? 11

Why do we eat turkey on Thanksgiving? 12

Why does a bee make honey? 14

Why are there zoos? 15

How many kinds of horses are there? 16

Where did the Easter bunny come from? 18

How do flies walk on the ceiling? 19

How does a caterpillar become a butterfly? 20

What are freckles? 22

Why do we burp? 23

Why do we have belly buttons? 24

How did streets get their names? 25

What good are insects? 26

How did sandwiches begin? 28

Why does the moon shine? 29

What is a relative? 30

What is a dinosaur? 32

How did Teddy bears get their name? 34

Why do we have different color hair? 35

How do seeds grow? 36

What is a computer? 38

Why do bees sting? 40

How many different kinds of colors are there? 41

What is a hospital like? 42

What animals live the longest? 44

Why do we need vitamins? 46

What is paper made of? 47

What is pollution? 48

Who were the first people in America? 50

How many kinds of dogs are there? 52

Do cats really have nine lives? 54

Why am I ticklish? 55

How many countries are there? 56

How did Halloween start? 58

Mommy, what can I do now? 60

Who thought up spaghetti?

We think the famous Italian explorer, Marco Polo, discovered spaghetti. He found the long, squiggly food in China and brought it back to Italy. The king named it spaghetti. And now spaghetti eaters are everywhere because nothing's more fun to eat than funny, skinny, scooting spaghetti. Put sauce on it, catch a piece and slide it down—ffloop!

Why is the ocean salty?

We believe the ocean gets its salt from the earth. Rocks have salt in them. Plants have salt in them. And there is salt in the soil. The rain falls and washes the salt out of the soil and into the sea. Rivers wear down the stones and carry more salt into the sea. You don't taste the salt in rivers because it doesn't have a chance to collect in them. You do taste it in the ocean because the ocean has been collecting salt for millions of years.

Why do birds sing?

Some people think birds sing just to make pretty music. But singing is a way some birds communicate with each other. Birds sing to warn strange birds to stay away from their nests or territory. Sometimes they sing to attract mates or to comfort their mates while the baby birds are hatching.

Some birds are very famous singers, like the wood thrush, nightingale, robin and the little pet canary. But not all birds sing. Some make other sounds to communicate, like owls that go "hoot, hoot" in the night.

People who like to hear birds sing often build little houses and put out food so the birds will come and stay.

What is a falling star?

When we see bright lights moving through the night sky, we say they are falling or shooting stars.

But they aren't really stars at all. A star is a heavenly body that shines by its own light. A falling star is really a small, stony mass we call a meteor.

We cannot see meteors until they enter the earth's atmosphere. Then, friction makes them so hot, they glow with a beautiful, fiery light until they fall to the ground and burn out.

Children all around the world think falling stars are lucky, so that when they see one, they make a wish on it.

Why do we eat turkey

 The reason we eat turkey on Thanksgiving is to remind us of the Pilgrims who ate wild turkey on the first Thanksgiving in America. The reason the Pilgrims ate turkey was because it tasted good and was plentiful enough so everyone could have seconds.

When the first Pilgrims landed in Plymouth in 1620 they faced a very cold winter with very little food.

 But then spring came and their Indian friend, Squanto, taught them how to fish and plant corn and hunt wild turkeys in the forest. They had plenty to eat. So when autumn came, the Pilgrims wanted to thank God for His goodness to them. They decided to have a feast and invite the Indians. On Thanksgiving day Chief Massasoit brought unexpected guests—90

on Thanksgiving?

braves. They sat down at long tables and ate for three days!

Between courses the Pilgrim fathers and the Indians played games and ran races. The Pilgrim mothers and boys and girls cooked and cooked — Indian pudding, clam chowder, roasted corn, corn bread and nut stuffing for the big bird. The

Indians went home happy. And the Pilgrims stayed strong all winter in their 7 little houses. They had enough food in their 3 big storehouses to last until spring.

Now we celebrate Thanksgiving on the fourth Thursday of November. And remember how many good things we have to be thankful for.

Why does a bee make honey?

A female bee makes honey in a special stomach that's like a little factory. But first she goes to a flower for the same reason you go to the supermarket. The flower contains the raw ingredients of honey.

She sips the sweet flower juice called <u>nectar</u> up through her mouth—which is shaped like a tiny soda straw—down into her honey stomach where it becomes the most healthful kind of sweet a person or a bee can eat.

If she ate all this honey herself, she'd get too fat to fly. So she wings back to the hive to feed the baby bees a delicious treat called bee bread made out of honey mixed with flower pollen.

Why are there zoos?

Zoos are for you so you can see and get to know animals you don't meet on every street corner. Peacocks not robins. Pandas not pussycats. Camels. Cougars. Kangaroos. They all call zoos home when they aren't in their real homes in the wild.

And a good zoo is like home. It is airy and grassy with winds to cool off in. And zoo keepers serve just the kind of food each animal likes best.

A zoo protects the animals that are getting rare so they won't become extinct from enemies like forest fire and hunger and hunters.

And don't forget that animal animals are just like human animals. They do not like to be teased, or yelled at. When you go to the zoo it's important that you wear your best manners.

15

Draft horse

There are five main kinds, and the work a horse does tells you what kind, or type, it is. The draft horse weighs nearly a ton and can haul heavy wagonloads. But once it was a war horse and carried a knight in armor and wore armor itself, over 400 pounds of it.

The harness horse is for high-stepping in front of a carriage. Before there were automobiles, people bought a 'heavy harness' breed if they needed something proud and dignified to drive. The creamy white Lippizaner was bred especially to draw the carriages of the Austrian Emperor. If he had wanted a sportier ride he would have

Harness horse

driven a 'light harness' trotter or pacer.

horses are there?

Saddle horse

A <u>saddle horse</u> takes you riding or hunting. It is usually three-gaited. It will walk, trot, or canter when you tell it to.

A hunter is a horse that must jump, too, and have lots of stamina. Most hunters and race horses are Thoroughbreds which means they are descended from one of three famous sires brought to England in 1685.

A <u>stock horse</u> can stop, start and turn very quickly. It is the one work horse the truck and tractor can't replace.

Stock horse

The smallest and gentlest horse of all is the <u>pony</u>. If it is a Shetland, it may not be much taller than you are—from 38 to 46 inches.

No matter how big or little a horse is today, the first horse over 60,000,000 years ago was no bigger than a fox terrier. It lived in forests and browsed on leaves. It joined up with man right after the dog, the camel and the cow.

It is very fast. It had to be to outrun the wolves in those early days. It remembers everything. And it is rather timid. So when you go up to a horse, always remember to move and speak gently.

Where did the Easter bunny come from?

Long ago in Germany there was a folk tale about a bird who was turned into a rabbit. It was so happy with its new shape that it celebrated its first spring as a floppy-eared fluffy bunny by giving people gifts of something it knew how to make when it was a bird: eggs!

And to this day we love the idea of the bunny bringing eggs at Easter—chocolate and jelly eggs and colored real ones—to celebrate the re-birth of life in the growing-est season of all, the spring.

How do flies walk on the ceiling?

The plump little pads on all six of a fly's feet flatten out when it walks on a smooth surface and give off a sticky liquid that holds it to the wall or ceiling like glue. Fruit fly, frit fly, blue bottle, midge, mosquito, marsh fly, horse fly, house fly, gnat—all have funny fabulous feet. Squish-squish-squish-squish. That's a fly walking. Shoo!

How does a caterpillar

A caterpillar is a butterfly's baby and it grows in 3 stages—egg, caterpillar, chrysalis. The tiny egg is laid by its mother on a favorite leaf. Soon the tiny caterpillar inside chews through its shell and begins eating its leaf—and every other leaf around. It is very greedy.

It grows very fat, very fast. Its old skin gets too small and it has to wiggle out of it. A soft new skin is always ready underneath. This process is called molting. It molts 4 or 5 times in butterfly babyhood.

Sometimes it changes color and spots after a molt. But it keeps 6 real legs and all its soft baby legs to support its long back.

become a butterfly?

Then one day it loses its appetite and leaves its leaf. It goes looking up and down stems and stalks for a safe place to become a chrysalis. This will be its last molt. It gets a new skin and a new shape. It may look like a twig or a piece of bark. It stays quiet in its chrysalis for a long time.

Then one warm morning—pop!—the chrysalis cracks. And a gorgeous butterfly pokes out. Its wings are wet and rumpled at first. But soon it dries out and flutters off into the sun to mate with another butterfly. More eggs, caterpillars, chrysalids. The cycle never stops.

What are freckles?

Freckles are little brown spots that you can't wash off. Some people have them on their faces and other parts of their bodies.

Freckles are formed in the skin by a certain kind of coloring matter that we call melanin.

If your mother and father have freckles, you probably will, too. Sometimes you can get new ones by staying out in the sun, because the sun causes the melanin under your skin to make new freckles.

Why do we burp?

Maybe you ate or drank too much. Popcorn's burpy-making and so is soda pop. Or maybe you ate too fast and didn't chew every mouthful into tiny bits. Or maybe your belt's too tight. Then all of a sudden, sometimes before you can cover your mouth—b-u-r-p. Excuse me!

Babies burp after bottles. Everybody burps now and then. It's natural.

Why do we have belly buttons?

A belly button marks the spot in the center of your tummy where you were attached to your mother before you were born. You were linked to her—deep down in a special place inside her—by an <u>umbilical</u> cord. The cord worked like a kind of straw. For nine months food from your mother's body passed along the cord and into you so you could get big enough and strong enough to live by yourself in the world. Once you were here you didn't need the cord any more so the doctor tied it up and tucked it in. And there you have it still: a belly button, known in grown-up circles as a navel.

How did streets get their names?

Before streets had names, people had to say "Turn right at the old oak tree and follow the brook over the mountain." So they decided streets should have names. Guess what they named the road near the old oak. Oak Tree Road. By the brook? Brookside Way. On the mountain? Mountain Avenue.

Of course, some streets are called Avenues, Boulevards, Lanes and Ways. Usually, Avenues are big streets and Boulevards are even grander, while Lanes are little and winding, and Ways are even squigglier.

Of course, almost every town has a Main Street. It's usually the main or most important street. (Probably when the town was new, it was the *only* street!) Some streets, like Lee Avenue, are named for families who started the town. Others, like Roosevelt Avenue, for famous people. Others for what is—or used to be—on the street, like Windmill Road. What do you suppose is on School Street?

25

What good

Lots of insects, though not all of them, are very good. Bees, for instance, buzz-buzz-buzz from flower to flower, carrying the dusty yellow pollen plants need to make the seeds that make more plants. Without bees, we wouldn't have honey for our morning toast.

Silk worms are just as busy as bees. They spin fine, fine threads—some over 1000 feet long—that are used to weave soft, silk cloth.

are insects?

Other insects are important because they hold bad bugs to a minimum. The skinny green praying mantis thinks pesty flies and mosquitoes are delicious. The plump red ladybug helps farmers protect their crops from another bad bug called an <u>aphid</u>. She has them for her dinner before they can chew up the food we need for our dinner.

Some insects are also fun to watch: butterflies, fireflies, and hard-working little ants.

How did sandwiches begin?

A long time ago in England there lived a man called the Earl of Sandwich. One day he was sitting at his table writing. He sat there a long time and he got very hungry, so he asked his servant to put a piece of meat between two slices of bread and bring it to him. No one had ever heard of doing such a thing before. But it was the servant's job to serve. So he gave the Earl exactly what he asked for: a piece of meat between two slices of bread. It must have tasted good because the next time he asked for a piece of cheese between the two slices of bread. And the time after that he asked for a piece of chicken between the slices of bread.

And before you could say peanut butter and jelly, everybody was eating this marvelous invention—even the servant. But no one knew what to call it. So they named it after the man who thought it up. And forever after two slices of bread with anything in the middle was called a sandwich.

Why does the moon shine?

The moon is a huge ball of rock and dust and craters that has no light of its own. When we see it shining, we're really seeing the sun's light reflected on the moon. At very rare times the moon also shines by earthshine. Earthshine is light reflected on the moon by the earth.

Sometimes as it moves around the earth we see it as a big, round, gleaming silver balloon. Some nights it's just a thin squiggle of light. Sometimes it looks like it's only half there. But it always looks silvery bright when you stand in front of your house at night and look up at the sky.

And now that the astronauts have been to the moon, it's exciting to think that some day you might be able to go there, too.

COUSINS ARE ALSO FRIENDS

A relative is a member of your family. Your closest relatives are your mother and your father, your brothers and sisters. The next closest are your grandparents. They are your parents' parents. Your parents' brothers and sisters are your aunts and uncles. All their children are your cousins—which makes you a cousin too.

BABIES ARE NEW RELATIVES

Every time a relative has a baby you have a new playmate who is also a member of your family. Soon there are lots of young people who are your kinfolk.

relative?

Relatives keep adding up so quickly that the best way to keep track of them is on a family tree, with grandparents on the top and branches for everybody else to show exactly who is who.

MARRIAGE

GRANDPA GRANDMA GRANDPA GRANDMA

Aunt Betty Uncle John DADDY Aunt JANE MOMMY Uncle DICK Aunt Lee

COUSIN ALVIN COUSIN FRANCIE

YOU SISTER COUSIN PAT COUSIN DAVE

Dinosaurs were a kind of reptile that lived many, many millions of years ago, long before there were any people on earth. They belonged to the same family as the snakes, lizards and turtles that live today.

The world was much wetter and warmer then. It was a perfect place for dinosaurs.

The very first dinosaurs were only about 6 feet long. Then they began to change. Some dinosaurs stayed small, some grew into big, heavy meat-eaters who walked on their hind legs. Some began to eat plants. Some could swim in the water even though they breathed air like the other reptiles.

One kind of dinosaur was <u>Brontosaurus</u>. It was as big as two city buses. Brontosaurus had a tiny head and a brain that was only as big as a man's fist.

dinosaur?

Another kind was <u>Stegosaurus</u> who had bony plates on its back and sharp spikes on its tail to protect itself from other dinosaurs.

<u>Tyrannosaurus Rex</u> was the biggest meat-eating land animal that ever lived. Its name means "king of the tyrant reptiles." It was 30 feet long and its teeth were as long as your foot. It was not only the largest, but also the last of the giant meat-eating dinosaurs.

No one is really sure why dinosaurs died out.

Maybe the world became too cool. Maybe it became too dry. We do know that when the dinosaurs died, their bodies sank into the mud. As time passed, some of their bones, teeth and skin turned to stone. These are called <u>fossils</u>. Fossils are the only reason we know as much as we do about the wonderful dinosaurs and how they looked and lived.

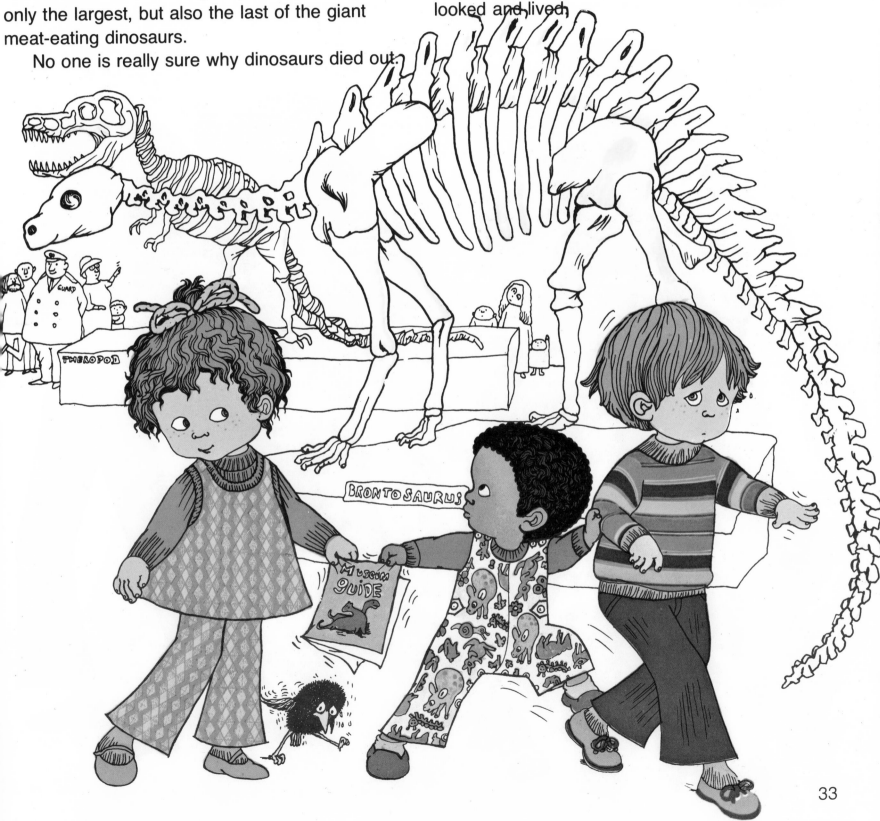

How did Teddy bears get their name?

They were named after Theodore "Teddy" Roosevelt, our twenty-sixth President and a great outdoors man. One day in 1902 on a hunting trip in Mississippi, he heard a commotion in the underbrush: leaves trembled, twigs snapped. The bushes parted to reveal—an adorable, roly-poly baby bear.

The President refused to shoot, of course. The story was drawn up into a cartoon and got in all the newspapers. And soon everyone wanted a Teddy bear like Teddy's bear.

All Teddies look pretty much alike: button eyes, a cuddly body, a plushy coat the color of brown sugar. He may be tiny or tall. He may squeak when you hug him hard. Or just keep smiling. But he is always very strong because any Teddy worthy of his name will last as long as you need him.

Why do we have different color hair?

Red or blond, brown or black, or in-between, your hair is the color it is because of <u>genes</u>. Genes are tiny but important parts of your body that come to you from your mother and father. A gene from each of them combines to give you every physical characteristic you have, including hair color.

Sometimes one gene is <u>dominant</u>—or stronger. When that happens, your hair will be the color passed along by the stronger gene. If both parents have the same color hair, chances are you'll have it too.

A seed is a tiny package with the makings of a whole new plant inside it. It grows in the spring when the ground is warm and the rain and temperature are just right.

 The spring rain drip-drip-drips down inside the seed coat. The sun shines. Soon the seed swells and pops open.

seeds grow?

Down go roots. Up shoots a leafy stem—right through the roof of earth. A plant is born.

Flowers and fruits and vegetables all grow from seeds and they make more seeds of their own. More daisies and buttercups, peas and limas, peanuts and pumpkins, apples and peaches, cucumbers and corn—there's no end to seeds.

A computer is a counting machine that solves all kinds of problems faster than the speed of light by changing them into numbers. It doesn't put down the numbers on a piece of paper with a pencil the way you do in school. It 'counts' with pulses of electricity. Each pulse takes only a few billionths of a second.

In one second a computer can do over 40,000 additions and subtractions. It can track a space capsule. It can even translate from one language to another if you program it with a dictionary and some grammar rules. New uses for computers are turning up every day.

 You can see how using a computer is a whole lot better than counting on your fingers and toes. Charles Babbage, an English mathematician, thought so. He designed the first true computer—complete with punch cards—over a hundred years ago. But the workmen of his day couldn't build it. We had to wait until 1946 when Americans at the University of Pennsylvania made the first electronic computer called ENIAC. It took up a whole big room. New

computer?

computers are smaller and smarter because they're built with midget transistors, smaller than the ones in the smallest television set. Some are no bigger than this dot ●.

Here are some computer words to know.

Program: Instructions to tell the computer what to do.

Programmer: The person who plans the instructions.

Punch cards: One way to feed a computer information. Square-ish holes are a code the computer understands.

Input: The facts and directions you put in.

Processing: All the counting the computer does to solve the problem.

Output: The computer's answer.

Memory: A box inside the computer to store facts.

Heart: Something a computer does not have and the reason it will need man always.

39

Why do bees sting?

Nature gives creatures different ways to protect themselves and their homes. Nature gave some little bees a very sharp sting.

There are many different kinds of bees. Some don't sting at all. But bumblebees and honeybees are two of the ones that do. The bumblebee can sting over and over again. But the honeybee can sting only once, because its stinger is pulled out of its body when it stings.

Some people are afraid of bees because they sting. But since bees sting only when they're frightened or hurt, they usually won't hurt you if you don't bother them.

How many different kinds of colors are there?

Nobody ever counted exactly—but there are at least a million colors. (Look around you right now and you can count quite a few.)

No matter what color you see—purple or orange, pink or brown or green—it comes from mixing the three basic colors called the <u>primary colors</u>: blue, yellow and red.

Take some paint and try it yourself. Yellow + blue makes green. Red + yellow makes orange. Blue + red makes purple.

And all the colors smooshed together make—black.

On the day you go to the hospital your mommy and daddy pack a little bag. Robe ✔
      Slippers ✔
      Toothbrush ✔
      Toothpaste ✔
      Favorite Toy ✔
The three of you walk up to a desk with a lady behind it. It's polite to tell her your name and how old you are. She might let you have a ride to your room in a shiny wheelchair.

Soon you're in your pajamas and sitting up on a tall bed with tall sides just like your old baby crib. You can see all the other children. Play if you feel like it. No yelling, though.

Everybody wants to know how you feel. The nurse weighs you and takes your temperature. The doctor thumps your chest. The lab lady comes around and pricks your finger for her tests—she's quick, like a mosquito, but nicer. Mommy and daddy

hospital like?

come and see you in the daytime. And nurses sit up all night so they can hear if you call them.

 And if you have an operation, you're special. You get a shot that makes you drowsy and another ride, this time on a bed with wheels. When you wake up, you're fixed up. Meals come on a tray. Get-well cards come in the mail from people who miss you. And soon they don't have to—because you're home and telling all your old friends how easy it is to go to the hospital.

What animals

There are over a million-and-a-half different kinds of animals in the world. But the ones whose birthdays are easiest to check are the vertebrates, or animals with backbones, like ourselves. A vertebrate can be a mammal (that's you), a bird, a fish, an amphibian (that's an animal that spends its life in and out of water), or a reptile.

Among mammals—and a mammal is usually an animal that has hair and nurses its young—man lives the longest: 113 years. Elephants come next with grandfathers of 70. A gorilla who takes care of itself can get to be 60. A lucky rhinoceros will reach 49. A horse is very old at 30.

Birds generally outlive mammals, parrots chat-

live the longest?

ting on till 100, eagles swooping and diving and seeing 80 anyway . . . 22-year-old canaries aren't unheard of.

A carp, 50. A halibut, 60. An aged beluga sturgeon that wins fins down at 70. How do we know? From growth rings on the <u>fish</u> scales and bones.

One famous pet toad lived with his adoptive family for 36 years. But another <u>amphibian</u>, the giant Japanese salamander, got to be bigger (5 feet long) and older (55).

Monster tortoises are related to dinosaurs and other more recent <u>reptiles</u> and live perhaps 200 years. But nobody knows for sure.

Why do we need vitamins?

If we want to have bright eyes and rosy cheeks, we need vitamin A.

If we want to have enough energy for work and play, we need the B vitamins.

If we don't want to get sick a lot, we need vitamin C.

If we want to have strong straight bones and teeth, we need vitamin D.

In fact, we need many different vitamins in order to live healthy, normal lives, because our bodies cannot get along without them.

Fortunately there are vitamins in almost everything we eat. To make sure we get all the vitamins we need, we should eat wholesome foods from each of these categories.

1) Milk, butter, eggs, and cheese.
2) Yellow and leafy green vegetables.
3) Meat, poultry, and fish.
4) Whole-grain breads and cereals.
5) Citrus and other fruits.

What is paper made of?

Most paper is made from trees cut down and sliced into tiny chips no bigger than postage stamps. The wood chips are cooked in a big vat with water and chemicals. The cooked mixture is called pulp and it looks like oatmeal.

When it's clean and de-lumped, it trickles through a long machine whose hot rollers squeeze the pulp flat and dry into a giant piece of paper 30 feet wide and hundreds of feet long.

Paper can be made from cotton fibers. Paper can also be made from paper itself. This is known as recycled paper and is very important to us, because then fewer new trees are cut down.

What is pollution?

There are many different kinds of pollution.
When factories or automobiles burn fuel and cough up dark clouds of smoke into the air, so that everything looks gray and it's hard to breathe —that's air pollution.

And when everyone in a traffic jam honks their horns until it hurts our ears, or when jet airports are built too close to people's homes so that loud sounds disturb their sleep—that's noise pollution.

And when cities pour their chemical wastes and garbage into our rivers and lakes, so that the fish can't live-–that's water pollution.

Pollution is unhealthy for flowers, insects, birds, fish, people and other living things, because we all need fresh air and clean water to live. That's why it is very important for everyone to stop polluting our world, and to start working together to clean it up.

Children can help, too, by throwing trash in the garbage can where it belongs. And children can help by reminding their parents to support pollution control.

Who were the first

The Indians were in America first, many thousands of years before anyone else. We think they walked from Asia and other faraway places over land and ice bridges at least 20,000 years ago. They settled all over this country from the Northwest to the Eastern forests.

In 1492 there were hundreds of Indian tribes. Families lived in sod huts, tepees, wigwams, wick-iups, longhouses, and adobe apartment houses called pueblos. But Indians were too busy to stay indoors. Some hunted buffalo for food, clothing and shelter. West Coast Indians fished for salmon and seal and gathered acorns for flour. Indian

people in America?

farmers were first to grow corn, peanuts and pumpkins.

Indians made everything they needed—tools and weapons, baskets and blankets, and beautiful clothes from cedar bark and buckskin. They loved to trade, too, and traveled hundreds of miles by canoe or by foot. All Indians believed in freedom and the rights of others. And they gave everybody everyday pleasures like moccasins and hammocks. Indian children learned everything from their parents and went everywhere with them.

EASTERN FORESTS

How many kinds

There are over one hundred breeds of dogs and six main groups—toys, hounds, terriers, working dogs, sporting dogs and non-sporting. Crossbreeds or just plain dog dogs are the biggest family of all.

Dog rules for people: Teach it to obey. It wants to learn. Don't hit it with anything. Love it and it will love you back as long as it can wag its tail.

Toy dogs are not as fragile as they look. They have big hearts and important friends. Montezuma kept Chihuahuas. The Pekingese was the sacred dog of Chinese emperors. Some Pekes were so tiny they could ride around in a kimono sleeve.

Mary, Queen of Scots, loved Toy Spaniels. The Pomeranian has husky relatives—the sled dogs.

There are more working dogs than any other kind. They pull sleds and little wagons. They herd sheep. They drive cattle. They help the police and guide the blind. They rescue people lost in the snow. They even give children rides. Collies, German Shepherds, Boxers, Great Danes, Old English Sheepdogs, and St. Bernards are all strong and contented: a dog with a job is a happy dog.

Hounds are gentle-hearted hunters. The hound family goes back 4000 years, so a hound may have been the original Dog. Wolfhounds, Deerhounds, Elkhounds, Foxhounds and Dachshunds, or badger-dogs are named for the animals they like to chase. Bassets and Bloodhounds have the best "noses" and the longest ears. Beagles are the best known hounds. A hound bays: Ooooooooooo.

# of dogs are there?

Spaniels, Pointers, Retrievers and Setters are all sporting dogs. And they have one thing in common: "bird sense." If there's a bird hiding in the bush, a good bird dog will find it. A Pointer will even point it out, standing in a straight line from nose to tail to show where the bird is hiding. Sporting dogs need room to roam and lots of exercise. Most don't care how cold or wet it gets. Some have built-in raincoats—very thick fur.

Non-sporting dogs are all very different from each other. Chow Chows are the only dogs in dogdom with blue-black tongues. The spotted Dalmatian is the fireman's special friend. Boston Terriers are the only true American dogs. There are oodles of Poodles, in all sizes and all colors—

even apricot. A Poodle's coat is a barber's joy. Its name comes from the German *pudel* and means to splash in water. It will if you let it.

Terriers are full of fun and fight. Almost all terriers came from England, Wales, Scotland or Ireland. They carry their backs straight and their heads high. They love to play and children are their favorite people. Bedlingtons, Kerry Blues, Fox, Airedales, Welsh, Irish and Scotties are famous terriers.

53

Do cats really have nine lives?

No, it just seems that way because a jump or fall that would hurt a person is nothing to a cat. It is so relaxed, rubbery and strong that it usually, though not always, lands on its feet. A cat can pussyfoot along spiky fences.

It can hear a mouse in its hole. It can see in the almost dark and guide itself by its whiskers. It can even retract its claws until it needs them.

A cat is clever, curious and no person is its master. Still, a cat truly loves its people family and is the only animal with a special way of telling them just how much, with its rickety-rackety purr.

Why am I ticklish?

Your skin is made up of millions of little receptors, or nerve endings, that tell you whether you're warm or cold or being touched by something. Some places are more sensitive than others because they have more receptors.

When something light and pleasant—like a feather or a blade of grass or a friend's tickling finger—touches your ticklish spot, all the little nerves in the vicinity tell the other nerves all along the line till your brain gets the message: kitchy-koo!

You can't help being ticklish any more than you can stop an itch or a sneeze.

So give in and giggle.

How many countries are there?

Right now there are 150 independent countries. But this number is always changing, as people who live in dependencies—colonies and territories that depend on the mother country for help —form new governments and become independent nations themselves.

A country can be a city (Singapore), an island (Malta), a whole continent (Australia), or just thirteen tiny struggling colonies that pulled together to become one big strong country stretching from sea to shining sea (the United States of America).

Independent countries, A to Z

Afghanistan	El Salvador	Liberia	Saudi Arabia
Albania	Equatorial Guinea	Libya	Senegal
Algeria	Ethiopia	Liechtenstein	Sierra Leone
Andorra	Fiji	Luxembourg	Sikkim
Argentina	Finland	Malagasy Republic	Singapore
Australia	France	Malawi	Somalia
Austria	Gabon	Malaysia	South Africa
Bahamas	Gambia	Maldives	Spain
Bahrain	Germany (East)	Mali	Sudan
Bangladesh	Germany (West)	Malta	Swaziland
Barbados	Ghana	Mauritania	Sweden
Belgium	Great Britain	Mauritius	Switzerland
Bhutan	Greece	Mexico	Syria
Bolivia	Guatemala	Monaco	Taiwan
Botswana	Guinea	Mongolia	Tanzania
Brazil	Guyana	Morocco	Thailand
Bulgaria	Haiti	Nauru	Togo
Burma	Honduras	Nepal	Tonga
Burundi	Hungary	Netherlands	Trinidad and Tobago
Cambodia	Iceland	New Zealand	Tunisia
Cameroon	India	Nicaragua	Turkey
Canada	Indonesia	Niger	Uganda
Central African Republic	Iran	Nigeria	United Arab Emirates
Ceylon	Iraq	Norway	United States
Chad	Ireland	Oman	Upper Volta
Chile	Israel	Pakistan	Uruguay
China	Italy	Panama	Vatican City
Colombia	Ivory Coast	Paraguay	Venezuela
Congo	Jamaica	Peru	Vietnam (North)
Costa Rica	Japan	Philippines	Vietnam (South)
Cuba	Jordan	Poland	Western Samoa
Cyprus	Kenya	Portugal	Yemen (Aden)
Czechoslovakia	Korea (North)	Qatar	Yemen (San'a)
Dahomey	Korea (South)	Rhodesia	Yugoslavia
Denmark	Kuwait	Romania	Zaire
Dominican Republic	Laos	Russia	Zambia
Ecuador	Lebanon	Rwanda	
Egypt	Lesotho	San Marino	

When you dress up like a goblin or ghost or witch or some strange, scary creature on Halloween, you are doing more than wearing a funny costume, you are following a tradition that has been going on in different ways for thousands of years.

The earliest we can trace it is back to the Druids, an order of priests who lived in ancient times in the lands that are now Britain, Ireland and France. They were very superstitious people who believed that on October 31st, all the wicked people who had died came back to earth, often in animal shapes. That's why we still see black cats, ghosts and cemeteries associated with Halloween.

Halloween start?

The Romans also had a festival about this same time. Every year they held a great feast to celebrate the autumn harvest. That's why we still use colorful autumn foods such as pumpkins and apples as Halloween decorations.

The name Halloween started in the eighth century, when the Roman Catholic Church declared November 1st as All Saints Day. The day before was a hallowed evening, or Halloween. The ancient pagan customs were still so popular, they were combined into this Christian feast day.

Our Halloween of course is very different from the ancient ones. Today instead of frightening people, it lets them have a lot of fun.

Talk on the funnyphone

Get a nice long piece of hose with no holes in it. Tape a funnel into each end. Talk into one while your friend listens. Then switch. No hose? Use two empty cans with a string connecting them through holes punched in the can-bottoms.

Make a mask out of a paper bag

Be a monster, a princess, a pirate, a cat, a mouse, or even your favorite storybook character. Start with a paper bag and cut out eyes, nose and mouth. Snip some ears out of construction paper and glue them on. Then glue or paint on eyebrows and mustaches and eye glasses. Disguise your voice. Give a play!

Make your own puppet out of a sock

Stuff top of old sock . . . paste on eyes and mouth . . . tie a bow around the neck. Get a friend to make one too. Name them and have a puppet show.

can I do now?

Grow a lawn

Sprinkle some lawn seed on a sponge in a plate that has a little bit of water in it. Then watch, and after a few days, you'll see grass sprouting. Bird seed is good to plant, too. Alfalfa from the health food store makes a nice plant. Any leftover seeds? Feed the birds.

Help Mother

Shell peas. Pull weeds. Break bread for stuffing. Straighten all the shoes in all the closets. Dustmop. Broom the front path. Help daddy wash the car. Set the table. Teach the baby pattycake. Put the pots away after dishwashing. Neaten a drawer. Put the little things—socks, ribbons, pins — in little boxes. Go through a magazine and teach a small brother or sister the words for things you see in the pictures.

Make a collection

Get some old magazines and look for pictures of people or animals. Cut them out and mount them on brightly painted, empty frozen juice cans. Now you can have a long line of friends on your dresser or your bedside table.